LEADERSHIP

A CHRISTIAN BASED MODEL CHANGING THE WORLD T.O.G.E.T.H.E.R.

EIGHT VIRTUES & PRACTICES THAT WILL MAKE YOU A GREAT LEADER

BY: PETER TASSI

A man who worked in one of Hamilton's giant steel mills, managed of over 1,000 men. He was well respected and loved by his employees. His virtuous character and practices transformed him from being a manager to a leader. When asked what the key elements of leadership were, he answered:

1. Get to know your employees as much as you can and respect them.
2. Always treat them like you would want to be treated.
3. Never forget where you came from.
4. Constantly thank them and reward them with compliments for work well done.
5. Thank them for your own promotions/success because they make you look good.

-Mick McBride

INTRODUCTION

Through my own career paths, I met many great leaders. It became evident to me that they possessed two main qualities; they were service orientated and virtue based.

When you're being inspired by great leaders, you cannot help but wonder what it is that they have that others lack. It was evident to me that great leaders were virtuous people and lived a service based life. I credit them for this model. It is my hope that this model will inspire you and provide you with the tools to be a great leader.

The importance of great leadership cannot be overstated. We need great leaders on every level and in every facet of life, doing their work healing, elevating, inspiring and empowering all of us. The effects of leadership are far reaching, shaping our personal and professional lives, our communities, the nation and the world. We crave great leadership. When hired, one of the first things we look at is our leader. Some of us seek out employment at a company primarily because of the leadership. Some of us will choose a less paying or even less favorable job because of leadership.

Great leadership requires much more than possessing a vast amount of knowledge and/or skills and experience. It requires acquiring the right virtues and executing the right practices. In this model, T.O.G.E.T.H.E.R. we will discuss the eight critical virtues and the corresponding modules/practices that will help you become a great leader. This virtue based model focuses on the development of your character and then putting this "new you" into action, executing the eight practices or modules.

I once asked a great man who possessed all the critical virtues, had a profound and enlightened view of the world and was a great leader, "How did you get the way you are?" He simply answered; "Hard work." Are you ready to embark on this path? Are you prepared to do the hard work? If you are, I am confident you will find the hard work well worth it.

CHOOSING A LEADER

"The more we serve our fellowmen in appropriate ways, the more substance there is to our souls. We become more significant individuals as we serve others. We become more substantive as we serve others—indeed, it is easier to 'find' ourselves because there is so much more of us to find."
-Spenser W. Kimball

I think that we can agree that the direction and well being of humanity rests heavily on the shoulders of great leaders. It is a heavy responsibility and requires a tremendous amount of personal work and development. Sitting on the right committees, saying all the right things, acquiring the knowledge and learning all the right nuances, may earn us a leadership position but, it doesn't make us a great leader. We may be politically savvy but we are not a great leader. We may have years of experience and fine tuned many skills, but this isn't enough. We will be skillful but not a great leader. To be a great leader you must acquire the right character and be a person of service and virtue.

Jesus never sat on the right commit¬tees, often said things that offended those in power and was not politically correct. He didn't have the experience or skills of a high priest but he was the embodiment of a service based and virtuous person. Consequently, he empowered us as individuals, re-directed an entire nation and changed the course of human history. It was no easy task for him and it won't be for you. But, you can do it!

It use to be common practice, and may still be with some companies, to reach out to their employees and solicit leaders. This involves a lot of work, but proves to be well worth the effort.

Today, we are more likely to subject ourselves only to the pool of ambitious people who apply for leadership roles. We should be looking beyond the pool, reach out to those who we believe have the potential to be great leaders. We have to reach out to them with enthusiasm and confidence and then facilitate the path for them to be our next leaders.

We want to do the hard work finding people who exemplify a service based approach to life and possess the seeds of the virtues required. We want people who are righteous. We want those who will not sacrifice in¬integrity. We want people who are not afraid of the hard work ahead, have passion for the mission and will approach it all with enthusiasm.

CHAPTER ONE

FROM MANAGER TO LEADER

"You can be appointed as a manager, but you aren't a leader till people choose to follow you."
John Adair

Parable of the Shepherd

"Very truly, I tell you, anyone who does not enter the sheepfold by the gate but climbs in by another way is a thief and a bandit. The one who enters by the gate is the shepherd of the sheep. The gatekeeper opens the gate for him, and the sheep hears his voice. He calls his own sheep by name and calls them out. When he has brought out all his own, he goes ahead of them, and the sheep follow him because they know his voice. They will not follow a stranger, but they will run from him because they do not know the voice of strangers."
John 10:1-18

Unlike most management positions, leadership allows you to inspire others, motivate them to find meaning and purpose in their work, and elevate them to a higher place. It allows you to impact the lives of others, serving as an instrument of change in their lives. You will bring to them a stronger sense of self, enriching their lives with purpose and meaning and empowering them to use the great gifts they have. You will have the ability to alter the course of their lives as well as the organization, bringing great success.
To be a great leader we want to build on the eight virtues of T.O.G.E.T.H.E.R.: Humility, Universality, Curiosity, Generosity, Respect, Empathy, Perseverance and Hope.

Corresponding to these virtues, we want to execute the eight corresponding modules/practices of T.O.G.E.T.H.E.R.: Transcend Self, Oneness of All, Greatness in Each, Empowering Others, Team Building, Healing Others, Executing the Vision and Realizing Results.

Leadership brings with it great stresses and challenges. Most challenging, is to become a better person; a more virtuous person. You have to say good-bye to the solitary life, working in your own isolated space, going home after work and forgetting about what went on all day. You are being challenged to greatness; to become the selfless, virtuous empowering force in the lives of your employees and your company. You are now intimately connected to everyone and it is your challenge to elevate each of them to a higher ground and accomplish the mission of the organization.

Consider the great works of the Sisters. They do not seek status, power, personal or financial gain. It's only the mission at hand that drives them to do the work they do. Their work is not easy. While working with the Sisters of Charity in the House of Dying in Haiti I said to one of the sisters, "This work is hard and filled with suffering and yet you left your country and comfort¬able life to do this work. Why do you choose to do what is most difficult?" She answered, "This is what God called me to do and I get great joy in doing what I've been called to do."

As it is with leadership- it will not be easy but if you do that which you have been called to do and be the person you are called to be, you will discover great success and happiness.

A wealthy friend of mine told me that wealthy business people shutter at the thought of a religious Sisters coming to their office. They know it will cost them a hefty donation because they find it impossible to turn down a Sister. It is much easier to turn down someone who asks for money who has their own personal interests at heart.

To turn down a humble Sister, who is focused solely on the mission, absent of any personal gain, is almost impossible. So it is with leadership. People get enthused about the mission because they see their leader working selflessly, with virtue, for the betterment of others and the actualization of the mission. Are you up to the challenge? Of course you are!

Jesus warned his disciples not to be like the rulers of his time. He warned them that if they are like the Pharisees or the rulers of Gentiles, ruling for their own personal gain and power, people will not follow them. People will act out of fear but not follow. He was clear that in order to be a leader, as difficult as it may be, we must become a servant first.

Because Jesus was the embodiment of everything he taught, his followers were constantly inspired and motivated. He didn't just preach the virtues, he was the actual embodiment of those virtues. This inspired his followers to change themselves and then go out and change the world. From just a few, billions of people over the centuries joined the crusade to accomplish this mission of service to build the kingdom. In spite of all the obstacles, including torture and death, they were not deterred from the mission. So, for those of you who want to be great leaders, you too have to do the hard work required of greatness; to embody the virtues and execute the corresponding modules/practices.

You have resources for greatness. You have probably read many books on the common belief that each of us has the divine within. This divine nature buried deep within the core of our being, is always seeking a way out. It seeks to surface and envelope our entire being. Taking on a leadership role provides you with the incentive to dig deep inside, to find the divine within you. When you do, others will choose to follow you.

CHAPTER TWO

MODULE ONE: (T) TRANSCEND SELF

"Those who find their life will lose it, and those who
lose their life for my sake will find it."
Matt. 10:39

TRANSCENDING SELF challenges us leaders to rise above ourselves. To succeed with Transcending Self, we will require the
virtue of HUMILITY.

Parable of the Pharisee and the Tax Collector

"Two men went up to the temple to pray, one a Pharisee and
the other a tax collector. The Pharisee, standing by himself, was
praying thus, 'God, I thank you that I am not like other people;
thieves, rogues, adulterers, or even like the tax collector. I fast
twice a week; I give a tenth of all my income.' But the tax collector standing far off, would not even look up to heaven, but was
beating his breast and saying, 'God, be merciful to me, a sinner!'
I tell you, this man went down to his home justified rather than
the other; for all who exalt themselves will be humbled, but all
who humble themselves will be exalted." Luke 18:9-14

Humility may be the most difficult of virtues to achieve. It involves reaching deep down, examining self and going through,
what can be, painful change. Humility is the seed for all other
virtues. It challenges us to rise above ourselves and free our¬-
selves of ego and selfish pursuits. Acquiring humility through
Module/Practice One (Transcending Self), is the way in which
we get ourselves ready for the journey and put ourselves in a
spiritual state to be a serviced based leader.

Personal development should be part of everyone's journey. We rise above our ego and our own self interests to be a person for others. We are challenged to leave our concerns for power, prestige, salary, bonuses and pension plans, to serve a cause greater than us. We are challenged to be a person for others.

Because attaining humility is so difficult, it should involve daily self reflection and asking if we have overcome our ego and selfish desires. Reflect daily on ways you can serve your employees, accomplishing the mission and attaining success for the organization. There are many ways in which one can do their regular checks: Daily readings, seminars, workshops and retreats are just some suggestions. Jesus, along with the great Greek philosophers and Christian theologians, are quick to teach that true happiness comes from living the virtuous/moral life and that life is born from humility.

When we focus our energy and dedicate our gifts in the service of others, we find true happiness. We have rid ourselves of envy or jealousy. When we shed ourselves of our "self," we are able to always act with courage and righteousness. We no longer have fear; no longer fear losing position, power or prestige. The process is a challenge but once accomplished, having humility, leadership is much easier. We no longer have anything to lose. We have separated ourselves from our own selfish desires and ego and are solely driven by all that is righteous; our goal being to empower others, serve the vision and accomplish the mission.

The paradox is that when we are no longer concerned with our own popularity we become more popular. The more we serve for the happiness of others the more happiness we experience. The more we relish in the talent of others, the more we are viewed as great. The more we humble ourselves and empower others, the more we are empowered. The more we distance ourselves from our own ego and serve others, the more others want to serve us.

One of the most inspiring leaders I have ever worked with was Father Lou Quinn, a Catholic missionary in the Dominican Republic. As soon as I walked into his mission and met him I believed I was in the presence of a saint. There was an aura and an energy that surrounded him. This bigger than life person, who mobilized hundreds of people to work and brought thou¬sands out of poverty, conducted his life as a simple humble servant. He would never draw attention to himself but work at serving and bringing the very best out of everyone else. His accomplishments were staggering, winning him awards from all over the world and making him one of the most revered people in the Dominican. Yet, he was filled with humility, seeing himself as a servant to those that suffered.

Fr. Lou certainly dared to walk that journey within and crush his ego, conquering all that would deter him from greatness. It is amazing how we can find the courage to parachute out of an airplane, cross the oceans in primitive boats, fight in war and do space travel, but not the courage to travel within. It's difficult to confront our weaknesses, the truthfulness to admit to them and begin the difficult journey of rising above ourselves.

Scenario # 1:

A leader asks an employee to work on a project and report his progress at the next meeting of the shareholders. The leader has been working on this for quite some time and has met with one obstacle after another, unable to solve the problem. With a few phone calls, using his connections as well as his negotiation powers, his employee solves the problem. He presents this solution at the next meeting. His leader is upset and pulls him into his office, ripping a strip off his back for embarrassing him in front of everyone. The boss claimed that this made him look bad in front of his shareholders. He told him that he should

have come to him first and made him aware of his progress.

The employee apologized and stated that it was not his intention to embarrass him or draw attention away from him. He actually believed he would be happy with his performance.

Should the employee have informed his leader of his progress in advance of the meeting?

Would this event cause a lost of trust between the leader and employee?

Would this action impede on future productivity of that employee and other employees?

Scenario #2:

During a recession, while many companies were laying off employees, a woman who owns her own company gave up a large part of her salary and corporate profits to keep her employees working and paid. She settled for a less luxurious lifestyle for herself and her family to make this happen. Her husband ,children and especially her closest friends did not think it was a good idea.

Was it right for her to sacrifice her existing family lifestyle?

Do you believe her employees would be truly grateful, causing them to be more devoted to the company and the mission?
OR
Are actions such as these taken for granted and soon forgotten?

Exercises:

Reflect on these two sayings on how they apply to great leadership.

"Power is of two kinds; one obtained by the fear of punishment, the other by acts of love."
Mahatma Gandhi

"The man who conquers a thousand armies is great but the man who conquers himself is greater." Confucius

Reflect on these words from Jesus. What actions and attitudes can you adopt that would have these apply to you?

"I have come down from heaven, not to do my own will, but the will of him who sent me." (John 6:38)

"Whoever wants to be first must be last of all and servant of all." (Mark 9:35)

CHAPTER THREE

MODULE TWO: (O) ONENESS OF ALL

"Never above you. Never below you. Always beside
you."
Walter Winchell

Module Two, ONENESS OF ALL, challenges leaders to bring
everyone together as one body. To accomplish this module, we
will require the virtue of UNIVERSALITY: the ability to treat
everyone equally, with the same level of care, love, esteem, ad-
miration and wonder. Everyone has the right to receive the same
treatment and not discriminated against for any reason.

Parable of the Lost Sheep

Now all the tax collectors and sinners were coming near to listen
to him. And the Pharisees and the scribes were grumbling and
saying, "This fellow welcomes sinners and eats with them. So he
told this parable: 'Which one of you, having a hundred sheep and
losing one of them, does not leave the ninety-nine in the wilder-
ness and go after the one that is lost until he finds it? When he
has found it, he lays it on his shoulders and rejoices. And when
he comes home, he calls together his friends and neighbors, saying to them, 'Rejoice with me, for I have found my sheep that was
lost.' Just so, I tell you, there will be more joy in heaven over one
sinner who repents than over ninety-nine righteous persons who
need no repentance." Luke 15:1-7

When everyone is treated equally and are viewed with the
same degree of wonder and awe, there develops a strong spirit

of co¬operation and teamwork. It is then that great things are accomplished. Contrary to the practice of his times, Jesus embraced the poor, the weak, the outcast, the disabled and the sinful. He also went against the grain when he gave women a place of prominence in his ministry. Women walked with Jesus and were considered as his disciples. He confided with them both privately and publicly. Sadly, an early patriarchal church ignored the role of women and gave them little if any prominence.

It is quite surprising to discover the status of the apostles Jesus chose. Even more shocking, given the time in history, was choosing women to be part of his inner circle. Women like Mary, his mother, Mary Magdalene, Mary and Martha all played an important role in his ministry. Further to this, Jesus speaks harshly and is critical of those who society believes to be in the upper class, who characteristically excluded many. He attacks them because they are the one's who place people on a level of importance based on their position, sex, wealth, civil and cultural status. As it turns out, it was the people Jesus chose, those in the lowest positions, that changed the world: fishermen, a tax collector, a carpenter, a revolutionist, a wanderer and women.

The famous theologian Dietrich Bonhoeffer wrote in his book entitled 'Life Together', "Though some division is purposeful, most is subtle, maybe even stirred up unknowingly. We often live unaware of how we act selfishly, out of self protection, with walls put up we might not see, and with self-centered motives." Are you guilty of this? I'm sure you don't do it knowingly, bu do you do it unknowingly? This is something we should always be reflecting on and checking ourself.

The challenge for us leaders is to rid ourselves and our staff of prejudices, biases and barriers that cause people to be divided or to be viewed as less important to the team. Placing people on a scale like a caste system seems to have always been a part of our history. As leaders, we want to develop a strong team through Oneness-everyone seeing each other as just as important, just as gifted, just as valued, bringing to the table a valuable contribution for success.

We have to put a wrecking ball to our ego. When we do this, we will value every employee equally and see the oneness of all. We have to dedicate our time and energy to every employee, valuing and respecting each equally.

The most brilliant and gifted people often come from the most unsuspecting places. All employees are gifted, capable of doing great things for the sake of the mission. More importantly, we are all one, not because we are all gifted but because we are all human.

I have worked in leadership positions and have been shocked to discover the life behind the man or woman who is the janitor, cleaner, delivery or warehouse worker. They lived a rich life, well beyond my own experiences and had acquired greatness of character.

Roughly fifteen years ago, they went on the hunt in the USA for the smartest people. They discovered that the two people having the highest IQ's were a man who was a bouncer in a bar and the second was a motorcycle repairman. When we look at any organization with open eyes and an open heart we realize that every member is part of the One that makes everything work.

In managing a real estate company and its holdings, I have had to hire and work with many tradespeople. I was surprised and sometimes shocked at just how brilliant many of them were. Some had higher IQ's than my university professors. I sometimes wonder how people treated or thought of Leonardo Da Vinci when he was organizing a banquet or a wedding. Da Vinci, considered by many as one of the greatest minds in human history, enjoyed organizing and decorating banquets more than many of his other pursuits. Was Da Vinci seen as a mere deco-rator or did people say; "I don't know that decorator but he may be the smartest man that ever lived."

While working for an organization, my colleagues decided to get philosophical and asked me; "Who do you believe was the most powerful person in the company?" I responded; "Harry the janitor." Our leader was not popular with the employees. When he asked for something, everyone only did, or pre-tend¬ed to do, what was barely necessary to escape his wrath. On the other hand, Harry was loved by everyone. Whatever Harry asked for, people would be eager to do. Truly admired and respected for his character and the virtues he possessed, he could mobilize people in ways that the leader of this organiza-tion could only dream of doing.

I vacationed at a resort in the Dominican. The people around the pool were talking about the colour of the wrist band they had and how different co lours represented different status on the resort, entitling each to different perks. To listen to the patrons talk about how some were more entitled than others based on the colour of their wrist band was comical as well as upsetting.

It doesn't matter who we are or where we are, we seem to be programmed to judge and categorize people on different levels of importance based on the position they hold and the wealth they possess. Is this part of our human nature? Is it written into our DNA?

The leader with the virtue of universality will acknowledge and lead in a way that recognizes every member of the team of equal value and infinite worth. They will lead in a way that empowers everyone in the same way, with the same amount of respect, inspiration and motivation given to each.

They will include everyone in the process, creating an environment that will facilitate cooperation. It will promote peacefulness among staff, never tolerating mistreatment of another. This environment of peacefulness and cooperation, equality and congeniality, stability and cohesion, will create a strong and powerful team that can accomplish any mission.

Scenario #1:

A leader has never given the level of respect to the employees in his company who occupied jobs considered lowly. He conducts his life and leadership style like a caste system. One day, he is confronted with a major problem. He has to resolve a dispute and it must be done quickly. He needs a translator. He surveys his entire staff and cannot find anyone who speaks Arabic. Finally, he checks in with the employees who work in the basement of the building, carrying out what he considers the menial tasks. He manages to find a woman who can speak Arabic. He calls upon her to translate.
Not only does she translate, she takes the liberty to improvise and add much to the negotiations. He knows this because his five word sentences are translated with a paragraph. Finally, everything is settled to everyone's satisfaction. He thanks his translator but is quick to take the credit with his staff and superiors.

Unfortunately, he would never venture into that basement to discover the wealth of talent: one of his custodians being a great artist, another a chess champion, the translator a great negotiator and a cleaning woman of outstanding character. Together, they formed a strong fraternity and family, able to overcome any challenge.

We may verbally take a stand against such practices, but then we quickly slip back to valuing people by the position they have and the power they possess.

Why is it that we always seem to be drawn back into a caste system mentality?

Scenario #2:

A senior management position arises. An employee is reluctant to apply, even though many of her co-workers encourage her to apply. It has a highly charged, aggressive male dominated executive. Even her husband is apprehensive about her applying. She is a gentle, mild tempered person, always exhibiting humility and kindness. In addition, she has no experience in management and lacks the knowledge that the senior executives possess.

Should she apply for the position?

Is her character, in the virtuous areas mentioned above, enough to be a great leader?

Does she need more experience and knowledge to do the job?

Should she become a more hardened and aggressive person to be a successful leader?

Exercises:

1. Reflect on these three sayings and write under each your thoughts.

"All differences in this world are of degree, and not of kind, because oneness is the secret of everything." Swami Vivekananda.

"Unity is oneness of purpose, not sameness of persons."
Tony Evans.

"Equality is the soul of liberty; there is, in fact, no liberty without it."
Frances Wright.

2. Reflect on these words from Paul's letters and think of ways in which you can make this part of your workplace environment.

"There is no longer Jew or Greek, there is no longer slave or free, there is no longer male or female; for all of you are one in Christ Jesus" (Galatians 3: 28)

"Agree with one another, live in peace; and the God of love and peace will be with you." (2 Cor. 13:11)

"Be kind to one another, tenderhearted, forgiving one another, as God in Christ has forgiven you." (Ephesians 4:32)

CHAPTER FOUR

MODULE THREE: (G) GREATNESS IN EACH

"There is greatness within everyone already. The job of the lead¬er is to make people discover and exploit the greatness already existing within them."
Israelmore Ayivor

Module Three, GREATNESS IN EACH, challenges every leader to discover the greatness in each and every employee. To accomplish this module, we will require the virtue of CURIOSITY; a deep and strong desire to know or learn about people.

Parable of the Pearl

"Again, the kingdom of heaven is like a merchant in search of fine pearls; on finding one pearl of great value, he went and sold all that he had and bought it." Matthew 13:45-46

It's a paradox that through finding greatness in others, our own greatness is actualized. Through elevating others to higher ground, we ourselves are elevated to greatness. Through actualizing greatness in the one, everyone is elevated and the mission of the organization can be accomplished.

Like many great minds in history, Thomas Edison was a handful as a child. He became a problem for his teachers who complained that he could not focus, was often distracted and caused mischief. They sent Thomas home with a letter to his mother saying that he would have to be home schooled because they could no longer handle him. Young Thomas asked his mother what the teachers wrote in the letter. She told him that they said he was so brilliant they could not teach him and he would have to be home schooled.

Every person has the potential for greatness because each has gifts and talents unique to them. We have to acknowledge and work hard to find it in our staff. The residuals will be great. For one of many possible reasons, many people have not yet discovered their greatness. We need to help them; to dig deep and find that greatness. Then we need to create an environment that will allow for their greatness to be actualized.

Finding greatness in each staff member takes a lot of work and time. We have to be insatiably curious. For many, curiosity is not a virtue they possess. They travel through life not asking the big questions. However, if you want to be a great leader, curiosity is a necessary virtue.

Finding greatness in another person also takes a leader who is fearless, willing to take risks. As a leader we are called upon to be mentors. Mentoring involves finding the best in each person and bringing it to the surface. With humility as our foundation, we believe in the greatness of others and act fearlessly. We are never threatened, fearful, jealous or apathetic. We are not deterred.

It is one of life's greatest fulfillment's: finding the greatness in others and elevating them to a higher ground. We get personal and professional satisfaction in seeing others do well. We relish the experience when we see others meet with success. And, of course, there is a great return on our investment. The employees will trust us, feeling confident and secure knowing that we are there to bring out the very best in them. This trust will manifests itself through undying loyalty and a passion to work and succeed.

We have to work at developing the ability to see below the surface, read be¬tween the lines, peer through the small window and see buried within another their greatness. In some cases, like with Edison's mother, we will see greatness where others see a problem. Do you have the ability to identify the gifts in others? Do you ever feel jealous when someone you work or live with has gifts equal or greater than yours?

If you do not have this ability, it can be acquired by rising above yourself, leaving behind your own ego and self interests. By creating an empty vessel within, you will now fill it with the greatness in others. If you find that you lack the ability to do this, don't hesitate to access others to assist you with this task. Remember, you are not creating greatness. It already exists. You only facilitate the discovery of it.

It sounds difficult and it is difficult, but an exciting journey to embark on. Imagine how much of a challenge it is and how much fun the process can be, spending a lot of mental and emotional energy looking for the greatness in others. You will engage with others in a new and joy filled way, saying to yourself, "I know there is something great in there, and I'm going to find it."

In addition to being curious, this process will require that you are charitable. Sometimes it is easier to write a cheque to a charity then pay a compliment to a staff member. It is easier to give accolades to a sponsor than it is to an employee. We have to be charitable in word and action. By discovering and revealing the greatness in others, you are giving them the added responsibility to live up to their greatness and to use it for the sake of the good of all.

Scenario #1:

A leader of a mission in Africa left for three months to work in his other orphanage in Lithuania. He left one of his long standing employees in charge of the mission. While absent, this appointee took over completely. He changed policies, contacted sponsors and asked for more money, extorting some of the money for personal use. When this came to the attention of the missionary he rushed back to Africa and took charge.

He offered his employee the opportunity to redeem himself. The employee apologized publicly in front of his entire community. The missionary re-appointed him a management role within a division of his mission.

Was the missionary overly concerned to bring the greatness he did see in this employee to the surface?

Was this a positive or negative message he left with his other employees and sponsors?

How does one judge when someone has crossed the line and needs to be fired?

Did the missionary see something in this person that others did not?

Exercises:

1. Reflect on these two sayings and write under each how you think it applies to you and what steps are you willing to take to "make it happen!"

"Be not afraid of greatness. Some are born great, some achieve greatness, and others have greatness thrust upon them." William Shakespeare

The test of leadership is not to put greatness into humanity, but to elicit it, for the greatness is already there." James Buchanan

2. Reflect on these words from Scriptures. Are you capable of doing this? What will you do to be this kind of leader?

"Do nothing from selfish ambition or conceit, but in humility regard others as better than yourselves." (Philippians 2:3)

CHAPTER FIVE

MODULE FOUR: (E) EMPOWERING EVERYONE

"The vision is really about empowering workers, giving them all the information about what's going on so they can do a lot more than they've done in the past."
Bill Gates

Module Four involves EMPOWERING OTHERS. Now that we have found greatness in another, we have to empower them. To accomplish this module, we will require the virtue of GENEROSITY. Being generous is putting the other person first, as well as being sympathetic, kind, warmhearted, complimentary and trusting.

Parable of the Mustard Seed

"The kingdom of heaven is like a mustard seed that someone took and sowed in his field; it is the smallest of all the seeds, but when it has grown it is the greatest of shrubs and becomes a tree, so that the birds of the air come and make nests in its branches."
Matthew 13:31-33

Empowering others has to be one of the most important actions we do as a leader. You have to do everything within your power to empower others so that the individual, team and company can succeed. The confidence you exude in others will give your team the encouragement and confidence they need to move forward boldly. When each person is empowered and trusted, the entire company will exceed expectations.

God recognized that the bond between him and his people was

something much deeper than a contract. It is described as a covenant. It is like a marriage, each loving the other unconditionally and doing all that they can to meet each other's needs and empowering them to actualize their greatness. Your relationship with employees is not a covenant, but it is deeper than a contract.

Covenant can serve as a model to search for the deeper relationship we can have with our employees. We take chances on them and when they fail we don't give up on them. When they act selfishly or use their gifts carelessly, we practice mercy. They may squander the opportunities we provide but, as long as they are willing to admit to their failings and try again, we offer opportunities.

After having discovered the gifts in others, you have to give them the tools, the autonomy and the opportunity to empower themselves. It is a risk. It may not always turn out the way you hoped. But overall, in the end, it will be a winning formula. When you empower staff, whatever the outcome, it sets the stage for something wonderful, in the person and the company. Who said that leadership wasn't risky.

As the leader, you are the one with the power, but you only have power to the degree that you empower others. When I presented this model to many young leaders, I asked them; "What is the sign of a great leader?" I was surprised at the number who replied, "The person who can empower us." Sometimes frightening and risky but empowering others will create an environment of trust and confidence. There can be no strong relationship between staff and leader if there is no trust. And, what better way to build trust then to empower them. What greater discovery then to provide the resources and environment for the gifts of another to be discovered and actualized?

We empower another human being by being complimentary, giving them responsibility, trusting in their judgment and even looking to them for direction. When we are generous with others it challenges us to surrender. We are called upon to surrender to something greater than us.

When we compliment another person, hold them in high esteem, reward them for great work, we hand our self over to them. This is a difficult thing to do. However, this kind of generosity is necessary to build strong relationships, to forge a strong team and to bring the best out of each person, empowering them to actualize their own gifts. Saying this, as important as it is to be trusting, we do need the wisdom to discern the degree of autonomy and latitude that we give.

Empowerment is not a gift or a privileged, it is a human right. This may sound radical. Every person has the right to be empowered, to actualize the gifts they have and to carry out their work with dignity, pride and a degree of ownership.

Until recently, life was very difficult. At one time we were nomads, spending most of our time hunting to survive. Then we became an agricultural people, living in one place, working the land day and night. Following the industrial revolution we began to experience more freedom in choosing the work we wanted to do. However, the work week was six days a week with ten to twelve hour days. Over the past fifty years or more, with emphasis on getting a good education combined with the technological revolution, we have more time and opportunity to choose what we do. We can, in the western world, for the first time in history, pursue the work we are more interested in and passionate about. This new world should facilitate more opportunity for people to be empowered.

Just as food, shelter and meaningful work is a human right, having the opportunity to explore and discover the greatness within is a human right. Imagine how many more Einstein's, Da Vinci's, Edison's and Tesla's there would have been if finding our greatness was a human right. This is for the betterment of the individual, the community, that nation and the world.

Scenario #1:

At the weekly management meetings the leader designates a list of jobs and duties to be completed by staff prior to the next meeting. This occurs week after week, the leader setting all the expectations and demands and the staff meeting these responsibilities. Fol¬lowing this, the leader reviews every detail, to be sure that the job was done to their specifications. Tasks given, tasks completed.

Is this a good practice of a leader?

How would you describe this kind of leadership?

Scenario #2:

It is a major violation for a night shift worker to fall asleep during the night shift. An employee working the night gets all his work done quickly and perfectly. The boredom is so over¬whelming over the remaining hours he constantly falls asleep. The leader catches him doing this a couple of times, reprimanding him and writing him up.

Is that how you would handle this situation? If not, what would you do differently?

Exercises:

1. Reflect on these two sayings and write under each how you think it applies to you and what steps are you willing to take to "make it happen!"

"We shine bright so that others may shine brighter."
Yohance Salimu

"Most people think that leadership is about being in charge. Most people think that leadership is about having all the answers and being the most intelligent or the most qualified person in the room. The irony is that it is the complete opposite. Leadership is about empowering others to achieve things they did not think possible. Leadership is about pointing in the direction, articulating a vision of the world that does no yet exist. Then asking help from others to insure that vision happens."
Simon Sinek

2. Reflect on these words from Jesus and write your thoughts. Are you willing to take the risk Jesus took?

"And I tell you, you are Peter, and on this rock I will build my church, and all the gates of Hades will not prevail against it. I will give you the keys of the kingdom of heaven, and whatever you bind on earth will be bound in heaven, and whatever you loose on earth will be loosed in heaven. (Matthew 16: 18-19)

"You did not choose me but I chose you. And I appointed you to go and bear fruit, fruit that will last, so that the Father will give you whenever you ask him in my name." (John 15:1)

CHAPTER SIX
MODULE FIVE: (T) TEAM BUILDING

"Coming together is a beginning. Keeping together is progress. Working together is success."
Henry Ford

Module Five involves TEAM BUILDING. This is a key ingredient to individual and corporate success. The virtue required here is RESPECT.

When you share your knowledge and experiences it demonstrates that you respect your employees. You trust them with what you have passed on and that they will use it to better themselves and others. This develops a powerful team. There should be no trade secrets!

The Parable of the Prodigal Son and His Brother

"There was a man who had two sons. The younger of them said to his father, 'Father, give me the share of the property that will belong to me.' So he divided his property between them. A few days later the younger son gathered all he head and traveled to a distant country, and there is a squandered his property in dissolute living. When he had spent everything, a sever famine took place throughout that country, and he began to be in need. So he went and hired himself out to one of the citizens of that country, who sent him to his fields to feed the pigs. He would gladly have filled himself with the pods that the pigs were eating; and no one gave him anything. But when he came to himself he said, 'How many of my father's hired hands have bread enough and to spare, but where I am dying of hunger!

I will get up and go to my father, and I will say to him, "Father, I have sinned against heaven and before you; I am no longer worthy to be called your son; treat me lie one of your hired hands." So he set off and went to his father. But while he was still far off, his father saw him and was filled with compassion; he ran and put his arms around him and kissed him. Then the son said to him, 'father, I have sinned against heaven and before you; I am no longer worthy to be called your son.' But the father said to his slaves, 'Quickly, bring out a robe-the best one-and put it on him; put a ring on his finger and sandals on his feet. And get the fated calf and kill it, and let us eat and celebrate; for this son of mine was dead and is alive again; he was lost and is found!' and they began to celebrate." Luke 15:11-24

Reach out and discover what your employees want to learn and facilitate their education. Realize that whenever someone learns something new there will be mistakes. Use these moments to educate and facilitate growth. And, as discussed, all employees must be treated with the same level of respect.

Important to building a strong team, we should keep in mind other important virtues and attitudes. As a leader we have to remain positive. A positive attitude works wonders in the lives of others. It's easy to become negative in our personal and professional life. It is very difficult to motivate others and inject them with ongoing energy if there is negativity.. We must maintain a positive attitude with cheerfulness. How many people do you know that are cheerful? Cheerfulness is powerful and works wonders. It brings people together. Cheerfulness motivates people, creating an atmosphere where they enjoy working with each other.

Working with the Sisters of Charity in Haiti or the Sisters of the Holy Trinity in Mexico I never knew who was the superior. There is such respect for each other, they are all equal and melt together as a homogeneous team.

They are so focused on the mission, you would have to ask them or listen intently to discern who the leader was. Whether I was sharing a meal, working or praying with them, I never knew who was in charge. Perhaps the great level of respect they had for each other was part of what made them so effective.

Jesus chose many candidates that would never be called back for a second interview in today's world. He saw something in them that was special. Perhaps, one of the characteristics was the ability of these candidates to put aside their own self interests for the purpose of service and achieving some¬thing great. Perhaps he saw that they had the temperament and disposition to work together.

There is a saying in sports, "A team is only as strong as its bench." In order to be a winning team, each and every player is valued. No matter if you are on the bench or on the field, winning teams have a profound respect for every member of the team. This attitude will build a powerful and unbeatable team.

People who believe in a common mission and have a leader who embodies that mission, find it easier to overcome differences and disagreements.. When respect is at the forefront, differences and disagreements are easy to overcome. As a strong leader, it is your job to instill respect, encouraging flexibility and the willingness to compromise. It is your job to create an environment that will produce a strong team.

You will often see in the world of sports, a team winning against teams that are much stronger. How does a less talented team beat a more talented team? This is accomplished through team¬work. A winning team bring with them a thirst that cannot be quenched, a spirit that will not damper and a likeness of mind. It's as if the members of these winning teams can read each other's mind. They and know the moves their teammates will make in the execution of every play. There is a unity and cohesion. It's as if there is a spiritual bond.

Jesus built a powerful team. Although a number of them were fishermen, there were others who had nothing in common. Mathew was a tax collector and Simon a zealot, both on opposite sides of the political spectrum. As previously mentioned, Jesus saw in those he chose qualities that would contribute to each other and work well in building his kingdom on earth.

When a leader inherits a team that doesn't exemplify these qualities he/she has quite a task on their hands. It's not easy to take a divided staff, or a staff that operates with strong cliques and create a powerful team. But, it is possible. A good lead¬er will exercise the virtues of respect, gratitude and loyalty to accomplish the mission. Grateful for each and every person and loyal to all its members, in spite of any differences. No matter the friction or lack of personal chemistry with an employee, we are challenged to take that extra step and to show each member the gratitude we have for their special talents and their contribution to the team. We set the example for the team through our own virtues and practices, inspiring others to strive for a homogeneous unit.

Our sense of purpose and meaning and even our own well being will not come from ourselves, but from serving people other than us and a cause greater than us. So, it is your job as a leader, to keep your staff focused on the mission and to show them, that through coming together, complimenting each other, respecting each other, loyal and grateful for each other, the mission will be accomplished. Even the impossible can be made possible.
A leader will demonstrate loyalty. Again, it is difficult to exercise the virtue of loyalty to members on the team a leader may be at odds with. But, it is necessary for a leader to show faithfulness and commitment to the people on the team, as well as

to their ideas. There is no better way than to win over a person than to show them that, in spite of a personality clash or differences, you are fiercely loyal to them and their own unique contributions.

It can be difficult to respect every employee equally, especially when some of your employees are at odds with you. No matter how difficult it is, a great leader will show respect equally to every team member. No matter how difficult it may be, every member of the team has to be treated with the same degree of dignity, courtesy and respect.

As a leader, never be afraid to put virtue and righteousness ahead of what society, shareholders, competitors or the status quo tells you. And remember, be willing to compromise all things except your integrity.

Scenario #1:

At staff meetings and through memos, a leader continually holds up one specific group of employees as doing outstanding work. Their work is outstanding and serves as a model of commitment to the company and mission, but they are always used as the model to follow.

Is this practice inspiring and empowering to the staff at large? Would you do the same? If not, what would you do different?

Scenario #2:

A leader sometimes changes his clothes at work, putting on casual attire. He is witnessed helping the janitor dispose of the garbage, relieve a worker for a short period to do his work for him, and carrying out some menial tasks left for the employees.

Does this behavior empower others or is it demeaning to the leadership role?

Will employees respect this leader more or less?

Scenario#3:

A boss leaves a note in employees mailbox on a Tuesday morning that he would like to meet with him on a Thursday afternoon.

Although this note may have good intentions, is it respectful?

How might employees respond to situations such as these?
Exercises:

1. Reflect and comment on these two sayings ?

"None of us is as smart as all of us."
Ken Blanchard

"Together, ordinary people can achieve extraordinary results."
Becka Schoettle

"It is amazing how much people get done if they do not worry
about who gets the credit."
Swahili proverb

2. Reflect on these words from Jesus and Paul and write your
thoughts regarding your leadership style.

"Be kind to one another, tender-hearted, forgiving one another,
as God in Christ has forgiven you." (Ephesians 4:32)

"Now I appeal to you, brothers and sisters, by the name of our
Lord Jesus Christ, that all of you should be in agreement and that
there should be no divisions among you; but that you should be
united in the same mind and the same purpose." (1 Corinthians
1:10)

CHAPTER SEVEN
MODULE SIX: (H) HEALING OTHERS

"The only work that will ultimately bring any good to
any of us is the work of contributing to the healing of
the world."
Marianne Williamson

Our mission for Module/Practice six is to HEAL OTHERS. In
order to be a healer one has to possess the virtue of EMPATHY.
One may say that a leader must conduct themselves in a pasto-
ral way. Yes, great leaders are pastors as well. Empathy denotes
a deep emotional understanding of another person's feelings
and/or problems. Empathy leads your employees to trust you,
confiding in you and comfortable in your presence.

The Parable of the Unforgiving Servant

"For this reason the kingdom of heaven may be compared to
a king who wished to settle accounts with his slaves. When he
began the reckoning, one who owed him ten thousand talents
was brought o him; and, as he could not pay, his lord ordered
him to be sold, together with his wife and children and all his
possessions, and payments to be made. So the slave fell on his
knees before him, saying, 'Have patience with me, and I will pay
you everything.' And out of pity for him, the lord of that slave
released him and forgave him the debt. But that same slave, as
he went out, came upon one of his fellow slaves who owed him
a hundred denarii; and seizing him by the throat, he said, 'Pay
what you owe.' Then his fellow slave fell down and pleaded with
him, 'Have patience with me, and I will pay you.' But he refused;
then he went and threw him into prison until he would pay the
debt.

When his fellow slaves saw what had happened, they were greatly distressed, and they went and reported to their lord all that had taken place. Then his lord summoned him and said to him. 'You wicked slave! I forgive you all that debt because you pleaded with me. Should you not have had mercy on your fellow slave, as I had mercy on you?' And in anger his lord handed him over to be tortured until he would pay his entire debt. So my heavenly Father will also do to every one of you, if you do not forgive your brother or sister from your heart."
Matthew 18:23-35

We have to learn to be active listeners, always able to manage our own feelings and emotions so that we can best heal others and solve interpersonal conflicts. Never hesitate to be curious and inquisitive, asking a lot of questions. To be a healing person, you have to be genuinely interested and dedicated to making a difference in the life of another. Spend with others the amount of time it takes.

Having the ability to feel what others are feeling and mitigate the situation is a real gift. We have to work at cultivating our virtue of empathy. When working through problems it may involve complicated calculating, analytical thinking and spending many hours with your employee. At other times it will just involve a few kind words. We have to always remember, leader¬ship calls us to elevate others to higher ground.

You will find healing others to be life altering. Sharing in another person's suffering and working at healing their brokenness is life changing. Not only does it build trust, comfort, confidence and loyalty, it will also change you. As difficult as it is, when we share in another persons suffering, we are transformed.
We often see broken people, after healing, end up being the strongest employees. They may also become better people, transformed by their suffering. You can feel good about playing a part in this process.

Many of history's most accomplished and geniuses suffered mental illness. Although we are tempted to run from these difficult situations because we fear them or believe we are not equipped to handle them, these are situations and employees we need to embrace.

I empathize with leaders who do not have the gift of counsel or the demeanor to deal with such situations. In these cases, at a minimum, they should have others on the team assist in healing. At minimum, they should be playing an active role in the process, playing some part in every step along the way. The important question here is, "What do we do with colleagues and staff when they are broken?" Do we use this as an opportunity to heal them, make them whole again or do we run from the situation. Do we become focused on the healing or do we become focused on ways of getting rid of the problem?

As leaders we will go through difficult times, make bad decisions and need the help of others. If we have not been patient and merciful to others, others will not be patient and merciful with us. If we heal others, they will heal us. In difficult times, employees will rally behind a leader who has shown empathy to others.

Scenario #1:

A woman on staff will not be a "yes" person to her leader. This approach often causes her trouble and anxiety. In addition, she is going through personal problems at home that lead her to having a mental breakdown. The company, not wanting to deal with her breakdown, decides to fire her on the basis of "restructuring," which is considered legal in some non union territories.

To what length should an employer go to heal another?

Does spending a lot of time, money and energy dealing with people's brokenness lead to an environment that is "too soft" and cause others to find excuses to avoid work?

Scenario #2:

An employee is in a deep state of depression and is suffering great anxiety. This is impeding on her work. She is medicating herself and often comes to work, although sober, with the smell of alcohol on her breath. Her boss has tolerated this many times over a long period of time. He now plans to fire her.

Is this a reasonable path to take?

Are there behaviors that are so outside what is acceptable that firing is the only option?

Scenario # 3:

A very gifted employee, brilliant at what he does, suffers mental illness. His illness expresses itself at work, often upsetting his employer and co-workers. When he is stable minded he is the most brilliant and gifted worker. When his mental illness shows itself, he becomes destructive to the team and the company.

What would you do?

Exercises:

1. Reflect on these sayings and write under each how you think it applies to you and what steps do you to take to "make it hap¬pen!"

"Whenever you forget self and strive for the betterment of others, and for something higher and better, you rise to the spiritual plane."
David O. McKay

"Our wounds are often the openings into the best and most beautiful part of us."
David Richo

Reflect on these words from Isaiah and think of ways, as a lead¬er, you can be healers.

"I have seen their ways, but I will heal them; I will lead them and repay them with comfort."
(Isaiah 57:18)
"O Lord, by these things people live, and in all these is the life of my spirit. O restore me to health and make me live! You have held back my life from the pit of destruction, for you have cast all my sins behind your back." Because you have cast all my sins behind your back."
(Isaiah 38:16-17)

CHAPTER EIGHT
MODULE SEVEN: (E) EXECUTE THE VISION

"Vision without execution is hallucination."
Thomas A. Edison

Module/Practice Seven, EXECUTING THE VISION takes a unique style of skills from a leader. To accomplish this module a leader requires the virtue of PERSEVERANCE.

Parable of the Persistent Widow

"In a certain city there was a judge who neither feared God nor had respect for people. In that city there was a widow who kept coming to him and saying, 'Grant me justice against my opponent.' For a while he refused; but later he said to himself, 'Though I have no fear of God and no respect for anyone, yet because this widow keeps bothering me, I will grant her justice, so that she may not wear me out by continually coming.'"
Luke 18:1-5

The people who succeed may not be the most intelligent or the most skilled. They convince themselves that they will get it done, no matter what. They usu¬ally have acute problem solving abilities and certainly have the virtue of perseverance. When confronted with a problem, they can find another path. One thing for sure, they persevere!

The Parable of the Persistent Widow is a great example of persistence. She knows that the judge will never see it her way and he will continue in his ignorant ways, unconcerned about justice. However, that did not deter her in getting what she believed to be just and right:

Many leaders understand the vision of their company and they believe in it. However, they lack the important virtues of Toughness, Diligence and Perseverance to execute the vision. They may crumble under pressure, give in to outside pressures, get bogged down in details or succumb to special interests. Their intention is good but they lack the virtues to carry out their intentions. Great leaders are focused, persevere in the face of adversity and are tough in character. They are steadfast, persistence and have great tenacity. They are determined.

Consider the athletic world. Some athletes are not born with natural ability and yet they make it. They persevered! They refused to give up. Rocky Marciano would be battered and beaten in points for twelve rounds but he would not quit. Face bloodied and body beaten, he would come out just as strong in the final three rounds, often knocking out his opponents. His perseverance earned him an unchallenged record in the heavy¬weight division of 49 and 0. How about the Cinderella Man, the story of James Braddock. He was not considered a great fighter, as well as being injured and aged fighter. However, he refused to quit and his perseverance won him the heavyweight title against the younger and more dangerous fighter, Max Baer. George Foreman, Col. Sanders, Grandma Moses are just a few who executed their vision and succeeded through perseverance.

Do what you have to do to execute your vision, overcoming and crashing through obstacles, pushing ahead to win the prize. Look at your situation topographically and when confronted by obstacles, find different ways and never give up. When your employees witness your perseverance, you will inspire them to never give up. They will jump on the moving train you have set in motion. They will become stronger workers, more committed and deter¬mined, having adopted your perseverance.

When you look at the life of St. Paul, you see a man who fought against, what seemed to be, impossible odds.

He was imprisoned, flogged, lashed, beaten and shipwrecked multiple times. In addition, he had to overcome problems and dissension in many of the church's he established. No matter what obstacles Paul confronted, he overcame them because he would not give up.

When you persevere, your employees will adopt your passion, be inspired by your perseverance and energized by you. They will believe that the impossible is possible. They will see the Big Picture and overcame the obstacles.

There are many creative and brilliant people who have great talent and vision. They are the great inventors and people who create brilliant ideas and systems that can change the world. However, executing this vision is not always easy and requires a perseverance they may not have. This is why brilliant writers have agents, companies hire marketing firms and some executives have their own "bull dogs." Executing the vision requires unending energy and perseverance.

To be a great leader, you need perseverance. Nothing deters you from executing and accomplishing the mission. You are able to take this beautiful concept, this bright picture of the future and execute the plan and make it happen. Mother Teresa and Martin Luther King not only had the vision- they also had what it took to execute that vision and change the world. Thomas Edison not only had many brilliant ideas, but carried out thousands of failed experiments until he succeeded.

Employees will try and emulate their leader, adopting the virtue of perseverance to get the job done. They will come to understand that success does not come easy; it involves blood, sweat and tears. Only those who persevere will accomplish the mission.

Scenario #1:

A leader inspires his staff at every staff meeting. He reminds them of the vision and mission, the importance of accomplishing the mission of the organization and all the wonderful results that will transpire. He breathes life back into them and gives them the inspiration and confidence to do the job.
However, following every meeting he is constantly stalled by obstacles, set backs and disappointments. He gets discouraged, often putting the issues aside. But, at the next meeting he delivers the same motivating and inspiring talk.

What can this leader do to overcome this problem?

What are some of the virtues he can work on to overcome this weakness?

Should this person be in a leadership position?

Scenario #2:

The atmosphere is one of tolerance and acceptance for those who break the laws of society and the company. A principal of a school runs into an issue where one of his students is breaking every rule; coming late to class, often out of uniform with a neck and face decorated with tattoos and jewelry. The principal suspends him until he is willing to conform to the rules. Knowledge of this situation becomes public and that principal is now taking heat from the media, some parents and even his own executive.

Should this leader cave to pressure and make the exception?

Will his perseverance translate into stubbornness, setting a bad tone for the community?

Will his actions be viewed as exemplifying the virtue of courage and standing up for what he believes to be right?

Exercises:

1. Reflect on these two sayings and write under each how you rate yourself in having the critical virtues.

"It's determination and commitment to an unrelenting pursuit of your goal – a commitment to excellence – that will enable you to attain the success you seek."
Mario Andretti

"It's not that I'm so smart, it's just that I stay with problems longer." Albert Einstein

2. Reflect on these words from Scriptures and write your thoughts on the ways they inspire you.

"So let us not grow weary in doing what is right, for harvest time, if we do not give up." (Galatians 6:9)

"We boast in our hope of sharing the glory of God. And not only that, but we boast in our sufferings, knowing that suffering produces endurance, and endurance produces character, and character produces hope, and hope does not disappoint us." (Romans 5: 2-4)

CHAPTER NINE
MODULE EIGHT: (R) REALIZING RESULTS

"Tolerance and apathy are the last virtues of a dying society"
Aristotle

Module/Practice Eight is REALIZING RESULTS. To work through this module we need the virtue of HOPE: an expectation and confidence for continued success with new and exciting projects.

This module involves two parts. First, realizing and celebrating the results accomplished and secondly, moving forward to accomplish and realize even greater accomplishments.

The Parable of the Rich Fool

"Someone in the crowd said to him, 'Teacher, tell my brother to divide the family inheritance with me.' But he said to him, 'Friend, who set me to be a judge or arbitrator over you?' And he said to them, 'Take care! Be on guard against all kinds of greed; for one's life does not consist in the abundance of possessions.' Then he told them a parable: ' The land of a rich man produced abundantly. And he thought to himself, 'What should I do, for I have no place to store my crops?' Then he said, 'I will do this: I will pull down my barns and build larger ones, and there I will store all my grain and my goods. And I will say to my soul, 'Soul, you have ample goods laid up for many years; relax, eat, drink, be merry.' But God said to him, 'You fool! This very night your life is being demanded of you. And the things you have prepared, whose will they be?' So it is with those who store up treasures for themselves but are not rich toward God." Luke 12:13-21

It's a deep desire in us to better ourselves, to continue to grow and accomplish great things. However, after people have accomplished great things they can become apathetic, lazy and often unhappy. We may feel proud and content with our career but our journey doesn't end when we retire. As a parent we may feel pride with having raised our children but the journey continues, always helping them and dedicating ourselves to them and any grandchildren. The journey never ends. We have to continually look forward and see who we can serve and what we can accomplish next.

With the virtue of hope, we always look to a brighter future, in spite of all the success or failures we have had. With enthusiasm we approach every future day with the same level of excitement and vision as the day before. With prudence we never allow yesterdays success or failures to get in the way of tomorrow's possibilities.

Module eight, realizing results, challenges leaders to return to the core virtue of module one, humility. We will not fall into the trap of complacency. All our hard work, dedication and success does not mean that we are perfect. What it does mean, is that we have to remind our-self of what it took to achieve what the team had accomplished. After all the celebrating, accolades and rewards, the team has to get back to work so that results and success continues to be realized. Because a company or organization have done well does not necessitate further success. In fact, the bar for competitors has been raised so we have to work just as hard if not harder to continue to see great results.

How many times have we seen empires, companies, church's and organizations crumble after success. It's tempting to rest on our laurels. Edison is a good example of someone who never saw their life's work complete. With over twelve hundred patents, fame and fortune, he kept moving forward with enthusiasm and living in the hope of creating another great invention that would further change the world.

As a great leader, your mission is never complete, no matter how much success you may have had. It is important that you and the team recognize there are even greater things to accomplish. Great leaders recognize that it is not only results that bring fulfillment, purpose and meaning to individual lives and the life of the company – it is the fight, the grind, the everyday hard work that enriches our life. None of us are perfect and none of us achieve the ultimate goal. In spite of all our success a great lead¬er realizes that there are different and sometimes harder days ahead. We are a leader with hope; hoping that tomorrow will be as successful and perhaps better than today. We are a leader with enthusiasm; looking forward to each new day with a whole new set of eyes. We are a leaders with prudence; never getting stuck in today or yesterday, making wise and prudent decisions based on what will come tomorrow.

Scenario#1:

A leader brings out the champagne, gives big bonuses, buys ex¬pensive furniture, builds a big office building and believes that their success they now experience will continue forever. They get lazy and complacent. They continue, not with hope but only expectation. They expect that their success will continue forever. Their job is done and all they have to do is follow the same formula. They lose enthusiasm, prudence falters and they begin to make poor judgments.

Is this scenario an easy temptation to fall into?

Have you seen this happen with organizations and companies? What was the result?

Exercises:

1. Reflect on these sayings and offer your thoughts:

"You can't start the next chapter of your life if you keep re-reading the last one."
Anonymous

"After all, the best part of a holiday is perhaps not so much to be resting yourself, as to see all the other fellows busy working."
Kenneth Grahame

Reflect on these words from scriptures and write your thoughts.

"Beloved, I do not consider that I have made it my own; but one thing I do: forgetting what lies behind and straining forward to what lies ahead." (Philippians 3:13)

"There is nothing better for mortals than to eat and drink, and find enjoyment in their toil." (Ecclesiastes 2:24)

CONCLUSION

While working in the missions in Rwanda I asked Rwandans why, in spite of their desperate poverty, they were happy. They asked me to hold out the palms of my hands. As I did, they said; "When your hands are full of things there is no room for God. But, when your hands are empty, there is lots of room for God." We clutter our lives with things and thoughts that serve no real purpose. As leaders, let's create the empty vessel so that we can be filled with all that is good. Oh, what a great leader we can be.

What a great joy it was to work with Sr. Vera Komar in the streets and mountains of Mexico. She left a tennis career, at the height of her career, being in the world's top thirty tennis players, to join the Trinitarians. Oh how wonderful it is to be able to surrender to a calling and a cause greater than us. As leaders, we will fall to our knees and surrender in order to take control and lead.

About the Author

Peter Tassi

Retired teacher/chaplain, mission worker and writer.

NON-FICTION BOOKS

- "Cane Boy" Book Series Elite Lizard Publishing Company
- "It All Started With Lasagna" Friesen Press
- "365 Prayers" Twenty Third Publications, USA
- "500 Prayers," Twenty-Third Publications, USA
- "The Beauty Within," Morehouse Publishing
- "Greatness in Our Teenagers: A 10-Step Guide for Parents and Educators," Paulist Press, USA
- "My Three Promises" Daizey Publishing USA and Canada
- "Doing What You Love and Loving What You Do." Published by HWCDSB.
- "Hamilton Heroes: Tales of Adventure, Adversity and Heroism from World War II," Kiwanas Canada
- "Jesus, The 4 Gospels Harmonized and Re-told in a Whole New Way." Daizey Publishing

MUSICAL PLAYS

- Stage Musical: "Padre Pio,"produced by Classical Theatre.
- Stage Musical: "The Centurion" performed by STM Theatre Group and theatre groups in Canada, the U.S., France, Philippines, Kuwait.

www.ingramcontent.com/pod-product-compliance
Lightning Source LLC
Chambersburg PA
CBHW070942120626
46546CB00004B/1529